The Story of Winston Churchill

Author: Bob Italia

Published by Abdo & Daughters, 6535 Cecilia Circle, Edina, Minnesota 55439

Library bound edition distributed by Rockbottom Books, Pentagon Tower, P.O. Box 36036, Minneapolis, Minnesota 55435

Copyright© 1990 by Abdo Consulting Group, Inc., Pentagon Tower, P.O. Box 36036, Minneapolis, Minnesota 55435. International copyrights reserved in all countries. No part of this book may be reproduced in any form without written permission from the publisher. Printed in the United States.

Library of Congress Number: 90-082615   ISBN: 0-939179-78-4

Cover Illustrated by: Marlene Kallen
Inside Photos by: Globe Photos and Wide World Photos

Consultant on this Book:
    Phyllis R. Abbott Ph.D. – University of Wisconsin (Madison)
    Professor of History
    Mankato State University
    Mankato, Minnesota

Edited by: Rosemary Wallner

— Contents —

ONE — A Royal Birth 5
TWO — A Troubled Student 6
THREE — A Military Success 8
FOUR — Churchill Goes to War 10
FIVE — Churchill and the British Parliament...14
SIX — Churchill and World War I 16
SEVEN — Standing Alone in Fear 18
EIGHT — World War II................................24
NINE — The Twilight Years 31
TEN — A Final Word 32

Winston Spencer Churchill

— ONE —

A Royal Birth

Winston Spencer Churchill was born on November 30, 1874, in Blenheim Palace, England. The palace was the home of the Duke of Marlborough, Churchill's grandfather.

Churchill's father, Lord Randolph Churchill, was a member of the British Parliament. His mother, Jennie, was the daughter of an American millionaire. They lived in a grand home of their own. They enjoyed a glamorous aristocratic life.

After Churchill's birth, Lord and Lady Randolph resumed their hectic social life. They did not have much time to raise their young son. They left him in the care of a nanny, Mrs. Elizabeth Anne Everest.

Mrs. Everest loved young Churchill as if he were her own son. She changed his diapers, fed him, and watched over him when he played. She was always with him. Churchill saw his mother only on his nanny's days off. "I loved her dearly," he later wrote of his mother, "but at a distance." Young Churchill saw his father even less.

— TWO —

A Troubled Student

In 1882, Churchill's parents sent him to St. George's School in Ascot, England. His parents thought he was a troublesome boy. They thought he needed discipline. Churchill was on his own for the first time, but he was miserable.

"How I hated this school," he once wrote. "And what a life of anxiety I lived there for more than two years. I made very little progress at my lessons, and none at all at games. I counted the days and hours to the end of every term."

Since he hated St. George's, he was always at the bottom of his class. This frustrated him. Churchill was not stupid. He enjoyed reading. He liked learning about things on his own. But he did not like the school's strict and brutal discipline. Churchill was in constant trouble, and was always getting into fights with his classmates.

When Churchill became ill in 1884, his parents removed him from St. George's. At his next school, he took an interest in French, history, poetry, swimming, and riding. But he especially loved English and began developing his writing skills.

When he was twelve years old, Churchill's parents sent him to a public school in Harrow, England. Still, he did not do well in his classes. His parents began to worry about his future.

— THREE —

A Military Success

Churchill's parents thought he was a dunce. Churchill didn't have any physical talents. His interests were limited.

But there was one thing young Churchill did enjoy. Every time he came home from school, he would play with his huge collection of toy soldiers. Churchill would spend hours setting up regiments and divisions and planning military campaigns.

One day, Churchill's father watched his son playing with the toy soldiers. He asked his son if he would like to join the army. Churchill agreed immediately.

From that point on, Churchill's parents prepared their son for entrance into the Royal Military Academy in Sandhurst, England. On Churchill's third try, he passed the academy's tough entrance exam.

Lord Randolph wanted his son to join the infantry. But Churchill had a great interest in and fondness for horses. He joined the cavalry.

Classes at the academy were much different, but more enjoyable to Winston. He studied mapmaking, battlefield tactics, construction of fortifications, and military law. Churchill had finally found subjects he was interested in. He studied hard, and did well on his assignments and tests.

Lord Randolph was pleasantly surprised with Churchill's success at military school. He began spending more time with his son. He introduced Churchill to important politicians and dignitaries. For Churchill, life was never more exciting or enjoyable.

But on January 24, 1895, Lord Randolph died of syphilis. Twenty-year-old Churchill was devastated. He had thought he would have many years with his father. Now, that chance was gone.

One month later, Churchill graduated with honors from the academy. No longer a dunce, Churchill was ranked eighth in a class of one hundred and fifty. He was assigned to a cavalry unit, the 4th Hussars.

Later, as he reflected on what he learned about life at the academy, Churchill wrote: "Don't take 'no' for an answer. Never submit to failure. You will make all kinds of mistakes. But as long as you are generous and true, you cannot hurt the world."

— FOUR —

Churchill Goes to War

It did not take long for Churchill to put his military training to use. In 1895, he went to Havana, Cuba and reported on the fighting between Spanish soldiers and Cuban natives. Next, he went to India where British troops were fighting local tribesmen.

This is what he later wrote of that experience:

> "Suddenly, the mountainside sprang to life. Swords flashed from behind rocks, bright flags waved here and there. Loud explosions resounded close at hand. From high up on the crag, one thousand, two thousand, three thousand feet above us, white and blue figures appeared, dropping down the mountainside from ledge to ledge like monkeys down the branches of a tall tree. A shrill crying arose from many points. Yi! Yi! Yi! Bang! Bang! Bang! The hostile figures continued to flow down the mountainside, and scores began to gather in rocks about a hundred yards away from us. I began to shoot carefully at the men gathered in the rocks. A lot of bullets whistled about us. But we lay very flat, and no harm was done. We had certainly found the adventure for which we had been looking."

During that battle, Churchill was noted for rescuing a wounded man. He had killed four of the enemy who had been in his way.

In 1898, Churchill published his first book about his war experiences. Later that year, he traveled to Africa's Sudan. He took part in the last cavalry charge the British army made. The battle lasted five hours. Ten thousand enemy soldiers were killed. The British lost only twenty-five soldiers. The horrors of the battle shocked Churchill and changed his ideas about the glories of war.

He wrote of the battle:

> "From the direction of the enemy, there came a succession of grisly apparitions; horses spouting blood, struggling on three legs, men staggering on foot, men bleeding from terrible wounds, fish-hook spears stuck right through them, arms and faces cut into pieces, bowels protruding, men gasping, crying, collapsing, expiring…"

Churchill resigned from the cavalry in 1899. He had no desire to fight anymore. He tried his hand at politics. He ran for parliament that year, but lost. Now out of a job, he went to work as a war correspondent.

While covering the Boer War in South Africa, Churchill was taken prisoner by the army of the Boer Republic. He was sent to a prison. After three weeks, he managed to escape. When no one was watching, Churchill jumped onto a moving freight train. When it became dark, he jumped off the train and hid in some nearby hills.

Churchill inspecting his British troops.

There, Churchill met a man friendly to the British. The man hid Churchill in a mine shaft and then smuggled him out of South Africa on another train. His escape became front page news. Churchill was a hero.

When he returned to England after the Boer War, he once again ran for parliament. This time, because of his hero status, Churchill won the election. At the young age of twenty-six, he was famous. Churchill was about to start his career in politics.

— FIVE —

Churchill and the British Parliament

From the start, Winston Churchill was in trouble with other members of the Conservative Party. He disagreed with many of the Party's policies. Frustrated with the Party's refusal to make any changes, Churchill one day left his seat with the Conservatives. He crossed the floor of the House of Commons and sat with the Liberal Party.

In 1906, the British people grew tired of the Conservatives. They voted many of them out of office. Churchill was now a Liberal and he stayed. His power grew. He became president of the Board of Trade and then cabinet minister.

Churchill worked hard for social reforms. He helped to establish healthful living standards for all. He had much concern for the old, sick, and poor. Many of today's welfare systems are based on Winston Churchill's ideas.

In 1910, Churchill became home secretary. He was forced to deal with striking workers who had different ideas about social reform. When strikers rioted in Llanelly, Wales, Churchill sent in troops. Four strikers were killed. Many people blamed Churchill for the deaths.

Churchill did not believe in giving women the right to vote. This earned him even more political enemies.

— SIX —

Churchill and World War I

In 1911, Churchill was named First Lord of the Admiralty. This meant he had total control of the Navy.

Germany was beginning to cause trouble around the world. Churchill sensed a great danger from them. He began to prepare Great Britain for the worst.

He built a new fleet of ships. Newer, bigger guns were installed. Older ships were converted from coal burning to oil burning. By 1914, the British had the most powerful Navy in the world. But Churchill did not stop there.

Churchill learned to fly an airplane and realized the great potential for aircraft. He was convinced air power would be an important weapon in future wars. He installed machine guns on his planes. British planes were the first to carry torpedoes. Churchill even began to think about launching aircraft from the decks of his ships.

When war was declared in June, 1914, Churchill was convinced Great Britain was more than ready for the challenge.

But the war against the Germans did not go as well as Churchill had planned. Two ships and 1,500 men were lost in one battle alone. Confidence in Churchill was fading. His political enemies, seeing that Churchill was no longer popular, kept him from having any real voice in the parliament.

Churchill as Minister of Munitions, sitting in his early version of a modern day tank.

Churchill was disappointed, but not defeated. He rejoined the army and was immediately made a colonel in the infantry. His successes on the battlefield returned power to him. He was appointed Minister of Munitions.

Churchill came up with the idea for land ships, which were early versions of modern tanks. He had hundreds of them built. They were an instant success. Churchill also expanded the machine gun corps and strengthened the British Air Force. All of these efforts ultimately helped to bring World War I to an end in 1918.

Once again, war had made Churchill a hero. But now that the war was over, what would he do next?

— SEVEN —

Standing Alone in Fear

From 1918 to 1939, much of the world was at peace. During these years, Churchill stayed active in parliament.

When the Communists started a revolt in Russia, Churchill opposed their actions. He considered the Communist leader, Lenin, to be "the embodiment of evil." He urged his government to ship arms to the Russian forces who were fighting the Communists. Then in 1920, Churchill wanted to send arms to Poland so they could fight the Russians. But the dock workers, remembering the four strikers who had been shot by Churchill's troops, refused to load the arms onto the ships. Even worse, they threatened to strike if any more aid was given to Poland. The government gave in to the workers' demands.

When elections came in 1922, Churchill was removed from parliament.

To make a living, Churchill began to write again. This time, he wrote about his experiences in World War I. Four of his books were published.

In 1924, Churchill's political career was briefly resurrected. He was appointed Chancellor of the Exchequer. He was now in charge of the treasury.

Churchill ready to defend his country.

Churchill was not very effective in this position, and he was the first to admit it. By 1929, Churchill found himself out of politics again and back at his desk writing books. But he still kept an eye on the outside world.

As in 1912, unrest in Germany was growing again. Germany's new leader, Adolf Hitler, wanted to rearm his country. He wanted the return of territories taken from Germany after they had lost the first world war.

Churchill felt the same way about the Germans as he had years ago. He did not trust them. He feared they would cause trouble in Europe once more if Hitler's demands were met.

In a speech to parliament, Churchill said:

> "Equal status is not what Germany is seeking. All these bands of sturdy Teutonic youths, marching through the streets of Germany with the light of desire in their eyes, are not looking for status. They are looking for weapons; and when they have weapons, they will then ask for the return of their lost territories."

Churchill knew that Hitler was building a powerful air force that would soon be stronger than Great Britain's. This frightened Churchill. He knew what kind of power an air force could command. He knew the kind of destruction it could rain down upon cities. Churchill voiced his fears loud and often to his government. But his fears went unnoticed.

Adolf Hitler promised Great Britain's prime minister Neville Chamberlain that once Germany reclaimed its lost territory, no more demands would be made. Chamberlain, as well as the British people, remembered how horrible World War I had been. They were eager to accept Hitler's word of honor. But not Churchill. He called Chamberlain's acceptance of Hitler's word a "shameful act."

In 1939, the Nazis unleashed *blitzkrieg* (lightning war) against Poland. Hitler had broken his promise to Great Britain. He wanted all of Europe—including Great Britain!

Churchill was immediately reappointed First Lord of the Admiralty. He was also appointed to the War Cabinet.

Churchill had been right about Hitler. But he was not happy about being right. Germany was coming after Great Britain with its terrible lightning war machine.

Churchill was now respectfully known as Sir Winston Churchill.

— EIGHT —

World War II

On May 10, 1940, a defeated Chamberlain resigned, and Churchill became Great Britain's new prime minister. The British people knew that if they were to survive a war, they needed a military man in command. Churchill was the right man for the job.

"We shall not flag or fail," he told the people in an emotional radio speech. "We shall go on to the end. We shall fight in France, we shall fight in the seas and the oceans, we shall defend our island whatever the cost may be. We shall fight on the beaches, we shall fight on the landing-grounds, we shall fight in the fields and in the streets, we shall fight in the hills. We shall never surrender!"

D-Day, the invasion at Normandy, France.

With this speech, Churchill set the fierce tone with which the British would defend their country. But Churchill knew that Great Britain needed more than tough words to defeat the Germans. Hitler's army was powerful. The Germans had taken all of France in a matter of weeks. Great Britain needed to be strong.

This is how Churchill viewed the war:

> "Upon this battle depends the survival of Christian civilization. The whole fury and might of the enemy must very soon be turned on us. Hitler knows that he will have to break us in this island or lose the war. If we can stand up to him, all Europe will be free. But if we fail, then the whole world will sink into the abyss of a new dark age. Let us therefore brace ourselves to our duties and so bear ourselves that, if the British Empire and its Commonwealth last for a thousand years, men will say: 'This was their finest hour'."

Meanwhile, Hitler was planning to invade Great Britain. The code name for his plan was "Operation Sealion."

The plan was to destroy the British Air Force with Germany's own air force, the Luftwaffe. As soon as the British were unable to defend their skies, Germany would send its terrifying army across the English Channel and invade England.

On August 15, 1940, Hitler sent the Luftwaffe to Great Britain. The Royal Air Force had 1,500 fighter pilots when the battle for the skies began. By the end of September, only 840 remained. Yet the powerful German air force could not win the battle. Each time the Germans sent their planes in the air, the Royal Air Force fought them and turned them back.

This is what Churchill said of their heroic efforts:

> "Never in the field of human conflict was so much owed by so many to so few."

Hitler was mad because the Luftwaffe could not defeat the Royal Air Force. He sent his bombers to destroy London.

On September 7, 1940, over 600 German bombers began to pound London. These raids soon became known as The Blitz. The bombers caused massive destruction to the city.

As Churchill described it:

> "Night after night, ten thousand or twenty thousand people were made homeless; [it was a time] when hospitals filled with mutilated men and women were themselves struck by bombs; when hundreds of thousands of weary people crowded together in unsafe and unsanitary shelter; when drains were smashed and light, power, and gas were paralyzed; and when, nevertheless, the whole fighting, toiling life of London had to go forward."

The bombing only reinforced Britain's determination to survive.

On December 7, 1941, the Japanese bombed the American fleet in Pearl Harbor, Hawaii. The United States, with all its industrial might, was now in the war. The United States had already been sending supplies to Britain. Now it would send its mighty army.

In late 1943, Churchill met with the United States' president, Franklin Delano Roosevelt, and Russia's leader, Joseph Stalin. The three leaders planned a secret invasion of France. The invasion would drive the German army out of France.

The plan was called Operation Overlord. It was set for June 6, 1944—D-Day!

Churchill at his meeting with President Franklin D. Roosevelt.

The invasion caught the Germans by surprise. The German army retreated from the tremendous onslaught of firepower Great Britain and its Allies threw at them. On May 8, 1945, the Germans, with their leader dead and their army in shambles, formally surrendered.

Never had Churchill seen a greater day. And never had he been such a hero. Great Britain had survived the worst war the world had ever experienced, and they had Churchill to thank for it.

Dwight Eisenhower and Churchill inspect U.S. troops before D-Day.

— NINE —

The Twilight Years

With his greatest victory behind him, Churchill had little left to do. He was a military man, a soldier. He excelled in war, not in peace. He knew it and so did the people of Great Britain.

Only eleven weeks after the war ended, Churchill was voted out of the prime minister's office. As he had done so many times before, Churchill began to write to occupy his time. He wrote about the war. He won the Nobel Prize for Literature, writing's highest honor. He also took up hobbies such as painting and horseback riding.

In 1951, Churchill returned to power as prime minister. In 1953, he accepted another great honor, the highest his country could offer. Churchill was made a knight and presented with the Order of the Garter. At seventy-eight years old, he was now known as Sir Winston Churchill.

Churchill remained prime minister for two more years before he decided to retire.

In 1963, he became the first honorary citizen of the United States. And in 1964, he gave up his seat in the House of Commons.

On January 24, 1965, Winston Churchill, 91, died of a stroke. His body lay in state in Westminster Hall for three days. An elaborate funeral was held in St. Paul's Cathedral. As he had requested, Churchill was buried in a small country churchyard next to his mother and father.

— TEN —

A Final Word

All of his life, Winston Churchill was a fighter, a warrior. He gained much power through his military actions. Some of his contemporaries used their power for selfish and evil gains. But Churchill fought to keep his country, and the world, free. He remains a great man for all the world to honor and admire.